THE
PERSONAL
PERMISSION SLIP

The Self-Mastery Guide for Students

COACH DOMINIQUE

The Personal Permission Slip:

The Self-Mastery Guide for Students

© 2025 The Coach Dominique Brand LLC

All rights reserved.

For permission requests, contact:

The Coach Dominique Brand LLC

Email: info@coachdominique.com

Website: www.coachdominique.com

First Edition

Printed in the United States of America

ISBN: 978-1-7348162-3-5

"Do not conform to the pattern of this world, but be transformed by the renewing of your mind."

— Romans 12:2 (NIV)

CONTENTS

DEDICATION

A Letter to the Girl I Used to Be

You didn't know it then, but every time you felt invisible, misunderstood, or out of place, you were being prepared. Every moment you silenced your voice to survive, every time you shrank in a room just to be accepted, every tear you cried when no one checked in or noticed—it was all leading here.

You thought you were just trying to get through.
But you were becoming.

So this guide? It's for you.
For the younger me.
For the one who felt too much, but still showed up.
For the one who carried more than she said out loud.
For the one who just needed someone to see her.

This is the guide you didn't have, but always needed.
And now it belongs to every student who has ever felt the same.

You're no longer just trying to find your voice.
You're learning how to own it.

So to every student who feels like the world doesn't get them:
This is your reminder that you've always mattered.
You don't need permission to take up space.
You only need the courage to show up as you.

I see you.
I believe in you.
And I wrote this for you.

Coach Dominique

TO THE STUDENT HOLDING THIS GUIDE

Before you flip another page, I need you to hear me.

You don't need to change who you are to be powerful.
You don't need to wait to be chosen.
And you don't need anyone else's permission to show up fully, speak up boldly, and stop shrinking to survive or fit in.

This is where I need you to really lean in.
Drown out all the outside noise because in this space, it's just me and you.

I wrote this because I've been where you are.
I know what it feels like to silence yourself just to make it through the day.
To walk through school like everything's cool while your mind is spinning and your heart is heavy.
To feel like you're always holding it together for everyone else while secretly falling apart inside.

I also know what it feels like to finally realize this isn't who I'm supposed to be.
That's when everything changed for me.

Now I help students like you tap into the kind of confidence that doesn't fold under pressure, and the kind of voice that can't be ignored.

This guide is your personal space to do just that.
It's not here to lecture you it's here to help you level up from the inside out.

Together, we're going to talk about what's real. The parts people don't always talk about.
I mean tapping into how you feel, how you see yourself, and how to move through what you've been carrying.

But you're not doing it alone. I'll be with you on every page, showing you how to write your own personal permission slip and be the powerful person you are meant to be.

You ready?
Let's go.

Coach Dominique

HOW TO USE THIS GUIDE
(aka What This Is & What It's Not)

Let me be clear, this isn't a textbook. It's a mirror!

Whether you heard me speak in person during my Personal Permission Slip keynote, saw a clip online, or you're just now meeting me for the first time, this guide was created with you in mind.

If you've already heard the keynote, you know it's not just a speech—it's a wake-up call. A challenge to stop shrinking, stop pretending, and start owning who you are.

And this guide is the follow-up. This is where we go deeper.

But even if you didn't hear the keynote (yet), don't worry. This guide still stands on its own. And who knows? By the time you finish, you just might want to hear the talk that started it all.

Because here's the truth:
You don't need a microphone to realize you've been holding back.
You don't need a stage to admit you've been carrying a lot.
What you need is a space to process it, reflect on it, and grow from it.

That's what this is—your personal permission slip to stop hiding and to start healing. Most importantly, to show up as you authentically and unapologetically.

Here's what it is:

✓ A space to be honest with yourself

✓ A guide to help you build confidence, own your story, and speak up

✓ A toolkit to help you protect your peace and power

Here's what it's not:

✗ A lecture

✗ A punishment

✗ A waste of time

There's no "right" way to move through this.

Write in the margins.

Circle words that hit.

Revisit pages when life gets heavy.

Skip around if that's your style.

This isn't about perfection.

It's about progress.

QUICK CHECK IN: HOW ARE YOU REALLY SHOWING UP?

Before we go any further, I want you to check in with **YOU**.

Rate each statement from 1 to 5:

1 = Never   2 = Rarely   3 = Sometimes

4 = Most of the time   5 = Always

#	Statement	Rating (1-5)
1	I speak up when something doesn't feel right.	
2	I feel seen and understood by the people around me.	
3	I believe in myself even when things get hard.	
4	I know what makes me different and I don't hide it.	

5	I set boundaries to protect my peace and mental health.	
6	I bounce back when I'm feeling down.	
7	I'm proud of who I am becoming.	
8	I show up as myself even when others don't	
9	I don't shrink just to fit in.	
10	I know my voice matters.	

Total your score if you want to or don't. That's not really the point. This isn't about getting a perfect number, it's a mirror of where you are right now. Circle any statement you want to work on and put a star next to the ones you already feel strong in. Then I want you to come back to this page in a month and do it again. See what's shifted. What stayed the same, and what new version of you is starting to show up.

THE FIVE PRINCIPLES OF THE PERSONAL PERMISSION SLIP

This is where it gets **REAL** as we dive into what changed everything for me, the five principles? Each one is a permission you have the right to give yourself not later, not when life feels easier but right now. You don't need to earn it. You don't need anyone's approval.

This is your Personal Permission Slip, and these are the five things it's built on. **(LEAN IN)** This is personal. Every word I'm sharing with you in this guide is coming from a real place.

So, as you read, I don't want you skimming through like it's just another workbook.

This is me talking to you. Vulnerable. Real. Honest. With that being said let's get into these principles.

PRINCIPLE #1

PERMISSION TO STOP PRETENDING

There was a time I'd walk into school with my head held high, hair laid, new outfit, and new shoes to match trying to *look* like I had it all together. I smiled, laughed, and answered questions like normal. But the truth is, I still felt invisible.

I've always been known as the *"strong one,"* even now. The one people come to, the one who doesn't cry. So, I kept pretending I was good, because I didn't want to disappoint anybody, and I definitely didn't want them to see me struggle.

But all that pretending? It became heavy.

HERE'S WHAT I LEARNED

Pretending might protect you for a little while, but it also prevents people from really knowing you, and when people don't really know you, they can't truly support you.

We wonder why we feel left out sometimes, why we never quite fit in. But have you ever thought about it like this, if you entered a friend group pretending to be someone you're not, how can they possibly see or appreciate the real version of *you*? You can't feel whole in a space you stepped into under pretenses.

Let that sink in.

The version of you that's always performing? That's not connection, that's survival.

You don't have to perform and act like you're strong or brave to be respected.
You don't have to smile to be liked.
You don't have to hide your feelings just to keep the peace.

I remember getting to a place where I wasn't even living, I was performing. So numb to who I truly was, so disconnected from my own feelings, I felt like a walking zombie. Like I was having an out-of-body experience every single day.

Please hear me when I say this:
Your honesty is not a weakness, it's a doorway to healing. You never needed their permission to be YOU, just the courage to be seen authentically and guess what .... I SEE YOU and I am loving this version.

Let's pause for a second not just to breathe, but to be honest. I don't want you to just read this and move on. I want you to *feel it.* Think back to a time you wore a mask. I'm not talking about Halloween. I'm talking about a time you wore a mask that nobody else could see.

Why'd you put it on?
To hide?
To keep the peace?
To survive?

Now let's be real! Have there been moments at school, at home, in friend groups where you showed up as someone you *thought* people wanted you to be? Where you downplayed what you liked just to fit in? Where you smiled and acted unbothered when your heart was heavy?

Let's go even deeper:

- Why do you think you've felt the need to hide those parts of you?

- What were you afraid might happen if people saw the *real* you?

- Have you ever walked into a room and felt like you had to earn your place?

- What's something about you that you've been afraid to share, but you're tired of tucking away?

- What would it feel like to finally take off the mask and show up as your *authentic* self?

Now pause and really take a second. Breathe in and sit with those questions, don't rush through them, because remember life is a marathon not a race so go at your pace.

Prompt!
Write it down and name it.

- Who are you when you're not performing?

- What's one small way you can stop pretending this week?

(Maybe it's speaking up. Maybe it's asking for help. Maybe it's finally saying, "I'm not okay.")

Before You Flip the Page…

You just did some real work, and that wasn't light So before you flip past it or distract yourself, just *sit with it*. Nobody said this would be easy, but here is the reward…

You grow when you're honest.
You heal when you stop hiding.

So, give yourself props for showing up, for being honest, and for choosing *you.*

Now, when you're ready…**Let's flip the script.**

PRINCIPLE #2

PERMISSION TO FLIP THE SCRIPT

You ever realize you've been living by a story that wasn't even yours? Maybe somebody told you that you were too loud, you're too much, or opposite maybe they told you that you're not enough. Maybe, it's not people at all, maybe life just kept happening and now you assume bad things are always going to happen.

Sometimes it sounds like this:

- "I'm just not smart enough."
- "I'll never be as good as them."
- "They'll probably judge me if I speak up."

Sound familiar?

We all carry around stories, some were handed to us, and some we picked up after being hurt or let down.

But here's the truth:

Just because that's how it's been doesn't mean that's how it has to stay. I used to believe I wasn't good enough. Not because someone directly told me that, but because of how life kept showing up. I wasn't the loudest in the room. I didn't have perfect grades. I made mistakes. And slowly I started to believe that meant I couldn't lead. Couldn't speak up. Couldn't be *that girl*.

The story I kept repeating in my head sounded like:

- "They're going to judge me."
- "They're going to talk about me once I leave"
- "I'm not built like her."

But I had to flip that script.

Because if you're not careful, you'll spend your whole life living by a story that was never even true to begin with.

Here's the real:

- You are NOT your lowest moment.
- You are NOT a permanent failure.
- You are NOT who they said you were.

At any point, you can stop repeating the old version and start rewriting the one that aligns with who you're becoming.

That's what flipping the script is about, changing the way that you speak to yourself **ON PURPOSE.**

It's a choice.
A discipline.
A reminder that your voice has power.
And your thoughts do too.

REAL TALK MOMENT

Let's sit with this for a second, just me and you.

What's a negative story or belief you've been holding onto that no longer serves you?
 (Maybe something someone said. Or something you've told yourself.)

Seriously, name it.

I know that might sound funny, but hear me out...

For example, I named that little voice in my head that tries to talk me out of my greatness.

She's loud, judgmental, and always has something to say when I'm about to do something bold.

So, I gave her a name, **Sasha,** and every time Sasha tries to creep in with her negativity and fear, I remind her who's really in charge.

So, what about you? Have you named that little voice in your mind yet? After you do, I want you to ask yourself this:

Who—or what—have you been letting take the mic in your mind?

- Where did that belief even come from?

- Has it *ever* been true?

- How has that story been holding you back?

- If you let it go, what would change for you?

Because here's the truth nobody tells you, sometimes the biggest thing keeping you stuck is the negative story you keep replaying in your head.

YOUR MINDSET CHALLENGE: "REWRITE THE NEGATIVE THOUGHT'

We're about to do something powerful, you're going to rewrite the script *on purpose.*

1. The negative thought you've been believing:
(What's the untrue thought or belief that's been holding you back?)

_____

_____

2. The Truth I'm Choosing Instead:
(Write a new thought that empowers, not limits you.)

_____

_____

3. If I believed this truth every day, what would shift for me?
(Be honest, how would you show up differently?)

_____

_____

Now take it a step further.

Choose one simple action you can do this week that *matches* your new truth.

Maybe that means speaking up, applying for something, setting a boundary, or walking a little taller.

Action Step:

_____

_____

And when that negative voice creeps back in **and it will**, you remind it who you are now.

You don't have to be perfect.
But you do have to be *intentional*.

Flipping the script is a decision you'll have to keep making, but the more you do it, the more natural it becomes.

LET'S CHECK IN REAL QUICK...

That last principle took honesty and courage.
But I need you to *sit in it* for a second.
Don't rush past the work you just did.

Because when you start flipping those old beliefs...
When you stop letting fear write your story...

You don't just shift your mindset, you shift your power.

And now that we've gone inward, it's time we talk about something just as important.

Because even when you *do* stop pretending...
Even when you *do* start showing up authentically...

If you don't know your worth, you'll still end up shrinking.

Let's talk about it.

PRINCIPLE #3

PERMISSION TO KNOW YOUR WORTH

Let's be real.

Confidence doesn't always come easy. Especially when you've been ignored, picked last, misunderstood, or made to feel like your ideas didn't matter.

When people don't recognize your value...
It's easy to start wondering if it's even there.

I've been there.

I used to stay silent, and walk with my head down and honestly, I didn't even notice I was doing that until someone pointed it out to me. Here's the thing: I wasn't doing it because I didn't have something to say, but because I wasn't sure if my voice even mattered. I'd keep my thoughts to myself. I'd second-guess my ideas. I'd let moments pass me by, convincing myself that speaking up wasn't worth the embarrassment. I allowed people to overlook me, because deep down, I was still learning how to *see* myself.

But here's the lesson I had to learn the hard way, if you don't know your worth, somebody else will try to hand you a discounted version of yourself. And if you're not careful you'll accept it.
Not because that's what you deserve, but because it's what you've gotten used to.

And here's what most people won't tell you: You teach people how to treat you **before you even open your mouth.** Your vibe, your energy, your walk, your appearance, it all speaks before you do. So how are you showing up?

Let me break that down:
You weren't put here to settle.

- Not in friendships.
- Not in how you let people treat you.
- Not in the goals you set for yourself.

Knowing your worth isn't about being cocky.
It's about being *clear*.

It's the confidence to say:

- I'm not proving myself to anybody, I already know who I am.

- I'm not waiting for a green light, I know I belong in the room, on the field, on the court, on the stage....

- Even if they slept on me, **God never did.**

You were born valuable.

Not when you **"get it together."**

Not when you reach some imaginary level of perfection.

Right now, just as you are and the moment you stop waiting for people to validate that is the moment you start moving differently.

REAL TALK MOMENT

Let's be honest:

- When do you feel most confident in yourself?

- What's a negative thought you've believed about your worth, that you're finally ready to let go?

ACTIVITY: THE VALUE CHECK

Sometimes we carry labels, pressure, and expectations that were never ours to begin with. It's time to let go of all that and remind yourself what you're really worth.

1. What's something you know you're good at but you downplay or keep to yourself?

(Stop being humble about it. Say it with your chest.)

_____

_____

2. What's something you've accepted or gone along with just to feel included even when you knew it didn't reflect who you really are?

(Be honest. This is your space.)

_____

_____

3. **What area of your life are you dimming your light just to fit in or keep the peace?**

(It could be a friend group, a classroom, or your own home. Wherever it is, name it.)

_____

_____

4. Write your Worth Statement, something you can come back to when you forget.

"I am worthy of _____ because _____."

Take this Worth Statement and turn it into something physical: a note on your mirror, a lock screen on your phone, or a voice memo in your own voice. Because when you see your value daily, it becomes harder for people to make you forget it.

READ THIS BEFORE YOU FLIP THE PAGE:

If nobody told you today *you matter.*

Not because of what you do.

But because of who you are.

And the moment you **really** believe that?

The way you move, speak, and show up will shift.

So, before we go any further...

Stand in that.

Say it to yourself.

Then let's keep building.

Because we're not just talking about confidence, we're learning how to protect it.

PRINCIPLE #4

PERMISSION TO PROTECT YOUR PEACE

There was a time in my life when I thought love and loyalty meant always being available. If someone needed something, I was on it. If they were upset, I showed up. If they called, I answered even when I didn't have the capacity.

Why?
Because I thought that's what loyalty looked like. I thought being dependable meant never missing a moment. I thought being strong meant never needing a break.

But here's the truth I had to face:
You can't keep showing up for everybody else while ignoring what you need.
That's not strength. That's self-neglect.

And eventually, it caught up with me.

I wasn't sleeping well.

I had zero motivation.

I felt numb, like I was just going through the motions.

And when I finally started setting boundaries, people made me feel guilty for doing what I needed to do for my own sanity.

- "Why are you acting funny?"
- "You think you're better than me now?"
- "Guess I can't depend on you like I used to."

And for a minute, I believed them.

But then I realized something powerful: **they were never mad that I changed, they were mad they could no longer benefit from my lack of boundaries.**

Let me say that again for the people in the back.

They were never mad that you changed, they were mad they lost unlimited access to you.

Here's what I need you to understand:

Peace isn't something that just shows up. You have to create it. Guard it. And sometimes, protect it from the very people who say they care about you the most.

Being the "strong friend" doesn't mean being everybody's savior.

Being dependable doesn't mean being constantly available.

And caring for people doesn't mean abandoning yourself.

You don't have to be the therapist, the fixer, the counselor, and the emergency contact for everybody all the time.

- You are allowed to have needs too.
- You are allowed to take breaks.
- You are allowed to unplug without apologizing for it.

Boundaries are not walls. They're doors that remind people that you get to decide who gets in, and have access to you and how much access they get.

Real Talk Moment: Check Your Peace Pattern

Let's map this out. Think of your energy like a phone battery. You wouldn't let your phone stay on 1% with 12 apps running in the background, right? But we do that with our lives.

1. **What's one thing (or one person) that drains you, but you keep allowing it because you don't want to seem rude or selfish?**

   _____

   _____

2. **Where are you saying "yes" out of guilt, not alignment?**

   _____

   _____

3. **How do you know when your peace is off?**
   (Think: physical signs, moods, energy shifts...)

   _____

   _____

4. **What's one boundary you need to set to feel like yourself again?**
   (Be specific. Don't say "less stress", say what would *actually* help.)

   _____

   _____

Use the chart below to take inventory of what's draining you and what's pouring into you. This isn't for likes. This is for *you*.

Draining Me	Feeding Me
(List people, habits, places, even apps that exhaust you)	(List what recharges you—activities, people, moments)

After you complete the chart, answer this:

Looking at what's draining you, what can you release, reduce, or restructure this month?

(Yes. Boundaries *are* an option.)

_____

_____

Then ask yourself:

What's one thing from the "Feeding Me" column you can make more space for this week?

_____

_____

Because listen...

You don't just protect your peace once.

You protect it *on **purpose***, consistently.

PRINCIPLE #5

PERMISSION TO OWN THE ROOM

This one took me a while to get, because for the longest time, I'd walk into rooms and immediately start shrinking.

- Not because I wasn't ready.
- Not because I didn't belong.
- But because I was afraid of being *seen*.

I'd scan the space, feel the energy, and try to figure out who I needed to be to "fit in" or which mask to put on. And somewhere in the process I lost track of who I really was.

I'd second-guess everything:
My voice.

My ideas.

Even my outfit.

And meanwhile, I had all this power, all this purpose, all this *light* sitting inside me. But I kept it quiet, because I didn't want to be misunderstood. I didn't want to make anyone uncomfortable, and I didn't want to stand out "too much."

But hear me:

You can't be who God called you to be while trying to fit where He never assigned you.

You weren't made to shrink.

You weren't made to blend in.

You were made to *own your space.*

Whether that's the classroom, the group chat, the basketball court, the track, the stage, the art room, the cafeteria, or the comments section, *you bring something valuable to the table.*

You just forgot you were the table.

Owning your space doesn't mean being the loudest in the room.

- It doesn't mean trying to be better than anyone.
- It's not about perfection or popularity.
- It's about knowing who you are, and refusing to shrink to make other people feel secure.
- It's the quiet confidence that says:

"I'm not proving myself to anybody I already know who I am."

"I'm not waiting for a green light, I know I belong."

"Even if they slept on me, God never did."

- You don't need to wait until you're "*perfect*", there's no such thing.
- You don't need their permission.
- You don't need 100K followers, perfect grades, or a starting spot on the team.
- **You just need to show up like you know you're already enough...BECAUSE YOU ARE!**

And the moment you stop trying to blend in?

Everything shifts.

Final Reflection: Step Into It

We're not shrinking anymore.

We're taking up space on purpose.

1. Picture your highest self, the version of you that's fully confident, focused, and free.
What's one bold move they're making that you've been scared to do?

(Say it. Then commit to one small action.)

_____

_____

2. What's a version of you that you've outgrown, but sometimes still slip back into? *(Maybe it's the quiet version. The people-pleaser. The overthinker. Name it and release it.)*

_____

_____

3. What space in your life are you ready to take back?

(It could be your voice, your art, your story, your mental health, your friendships. Reclaim it.)

_____

_____

4. Finish this sentence:

"I won't shrink again because I now know

_____."

BONUS PROMPT: WRITE THE VISION

A Letter to My Future Self

You made it.

Not just to the end of a book, but through a journey most people never even start.
You looked in the mirror. You peeled some layers back.
You showed up for yourself.
Now, it's time to speak into the version of you that's still becoming.

This is your moment to pour into your *future self*.
The one who might forget how far you've come.
The one who might need a reminder that you don't have to be perfect to be powerful.
The one who still doubts their voice sometimes, but is showing up anyway.

So, I want you to write your future self a letter. Tell your future self what they need to remember.

Remind your future self what you're done settling for, and speak life over your journey, in your own words.

Because this is personal

YOUR PERSONAL PERMISSION SLIP

This right here?

This is the part where you stop playing small.

Where you stop waiting for someone else to validate your growth.

You've already done the work, now it's time to *own it.*

You don't need permission from your past.

Not from your school, your friends, your feed, or your fear.

From this moment forward, you've got permission to take up space and *be the real you*.

Sign this slip like you mean it.

I give myself permission to:

- Be honest about where I am
- Take off the mask
- Flip the script
- Own my worth

- Protect my peace
- Keep showing up as the real me

Not for them.

For me.

Because this journey…is personal.

Signed: _____

Date: _____

LOCKED IN

Let's close this out the right way.

You've made it through the hard stuff. You've reflected.

Unpacked. Told the truth.

Now let's make it plain.

This page?

This is your proof.

These are the truths I want you to come back to when life gets loud, when self-doubt tries to creep in, or when you forget who you are.

So, before you flip to the journaling pages... lock in.

Stand On Business:

Need help getting started? Here are a few to finish in your own way:

- I don't have to pretend to be _____ just to be accepted.

- I bring _____ into every space I enter.

- I'm not waiting for permission to _____.

- I'm allowed to say no to _____ without feeling guilty.

- I was created to _____, not shrink.

Now write your own truth below. Something you know about yourself no matter what.

_____

_____

_____

AFTER YOU'VE GIVEN YOUESELF PERMISSION

Living What You Just Claimed

This is the part where you go from reflecting... to applying.

You've done the work. Sat with some hard truths. Took the mask off. Told your story, in your words. But don't let this just be a powerful moment. Let it be a lifestyle shift.

Because here's the truth: Anybody can say "I'm ready to grow" when it's quiet and comfortable. But what happens when life pushes back? When the old habits try to creep in? When the people around you aren't growing with you?

These next pages are about the *follow-through*.

What This Section Will Teach You:

- How to stand on confidence even when you start to question yourself
- What it looks like to use your voice in real situations—not just safe ones
- How to protect your peace without guilt or over-explaining

- Why boundaries matter, and how to enforce them without fear
- How to stop settling for any space that doesn't match your value

This part isn't easy. It's not hype. It's about walking in the truth you just claimed. In real life. Every day.

Let's get into it.

CONFIDENCE CHECK – WHEN DOUBT CREEPS IN

Let's be real, confidence is easy when everything's going your way. But what about the days when you second-guess everything? When your voice shakes, your ideas feel too small, and that little voice in your head says "You're not good enough"?

Yeah, those days because confidence isn't the absence of doubt. It's the decision to keep showing up anyway.

You might've had to fight to believe in yourself. Maybe confidence didn't come naturally. Maybe you had to unlearn everything that told you to stay small.

But let me remind you of something:

Confidence isn't loud. It's consistent.
It's not about being perfect. It's about being present.
It's saying: "I may not feel 100 today, but I still know who I am."

Real-Life Reminder:

Your confidence will get tested. Especially when you start stepping into new levels, new spaces, and new versions of yourself. But tested doesn't mean broken. Shaky doesn't mean fake. You're just human. Keep standing.

Self-Mastery Check-In:

Finish the statements below in your own words:

When I start to doubt myself, I will remind myself that...

_____

_____

I feel the most confident when I'm...

_____

_____

I may not have it all figured out, but I know for sure...

_____

_____

When you're done filling this out, don't just close the book. Reread your words. Own them. That's what locking it in looks like in real life.

OWNING MY VOICE IN REAL LIFE

You ever walk away from a moment and think,
"Dang, I should've said something."
Yeah… that part.

It's easy to say "I'm gonna speak up more" when you're by yourself, but the real test? That comes in the hallway, the group chat, the lunchroom, the classroom, the house.

Real life. Real pressure. Real people.

When you've spent years silencing yourself just to survive, using your voice again can feel scary, awkward, or "too much." But let me be clear…

Your voice is not a problem. Your silence is not protection.

Your voice holds weight and not just the kind that gets loud in an argument. I'm talking about the voice that sets boundaries, shares ideas, asks for help, or says "That made me uncomfortable."

That voice matters.

Your voice wasn't given to you to impress people. It was given to you to make an impact.

Use it, even if your hands shake. Even if your voice cracks. Say what needs to be said.

Self-Mastery Check-In

Finish these in your own words. No filter.

One moment where I should've spoken up but didn't:

_____

_____

What I wish I would've said in that moment:

_____

_____

The next time something like that happens, I will...

_____

_____

My voice deserves to be heard when...

_____

_____

Keep practicing. You don't have to get it perfect. You just have to get more honest.

PROTECTING YOUR PEACE WITHOUT GUILT

Let's get something straight:
Protecting your peace is **NOT** selfish.
It's survival.

Too often, we feel bad for taking a break, setting a boundary, or choosing not to be available for everybody else. But guess what? Your peace has a price, and when you keep giving it away for free it costs you your clarity, your energy, and sometimes even your identity.

You're not here to fix everybody, you're not here to say "yes" to everything.
You're here to grow, heal and show up whole.

That starts with checking in with yourself, not checking out of your own needs.

Real-Life Reminder:

You can be kind and still say no.
You can love people and still create space.
You can care deeply and still choose yourself.

Self-Mastery Check-In

What's one situation that keeps draining my peace lately?

_____

_____

Why have I been tolerating it?

_____

_____

What boundary do I need to set to protect my peace?

_____

_____

What would change if I finally followed through on that boundary?

_____

_____

What would it feel like to give myself permission to rest without guilt?

_____

_____

You can't pour from an empty cup. You weren't created to be everything to everybody.
Protect your peace like it's sacred, because it is.

MY BOUNDARIES ARE NOT UP FOR DEBATE?

Some people won't respect your boundaries because they benefit from you not having any.

Let that sink in.

Every time you say "yes" when you really mean "no," you teach people that your needs don't matter. Every time you bend past your breaking point just to avoid disappointing someone, you abandon yourself.

That stops here!

Boundaries aren't walls, they're doors with locks. You get to decide who has a key
and if someone gets offended by the fact that you finally started choosing yourself, they were never for you in the first place.

Let's Be Clear:

- Saying "no" is not being rude.
- Taking a break doesn't mean you're lazy.
- Needing space doesn't make you dramatic.
- Protecting your energy is your responsibility not theirs.

Where in my life have I been too flexible with my boundaries?

_____

_____

What does that flexibility cost me—mentally, emotionally, physically?

_____

_____

What boundary do I need to reinforce right now?

_____

_____

What's one way I can honor my own needs this week without apologizing for them?

_____

_____

You don't owe anyone access to a version of you that's constantly overextending, burning out, or bending to fit. Your boundaries are not suggestions they're standards.

And they're not up for debate.

I DON'T JUST WANT THE ROOM...
I WANT THE RIGHT ONE!

What this page will teach you:

How to stop chasing access and start chasing alignment, because being "in the room" means nothing if you lose yourself just to stay there.

We hear it all the time...
"Get in the room."
"Take your seat at the table."
"Be where the opportunities are."

But what happens when the room wasn't built for you? What happens when you get there, but you can't even breathe?

Listen, I'm all for breaking barriers and showing up boldly, but if being in the room means hiding who you are, constantly shrinking, or begging to be seen you're not in the *right* room.

The right room affirms your voice.
The right room honors your truth.
The right room doesn't require you to hustle for basic respect.

And here's the part nobody tells you:
Sometimes you've gotta build the room yourself.
From the ground up.
Brick by brick.
Even if you're the only one in it at first, because peace is better than proximity and alignment is louder than applause.

Take This with You:

- Access is not the same as acceptance.
- Just because the door opened doesn't mean you have to walk through it.
- If you have to lose yourself to belong, you're not winning.

Let's Reflect:

Where have I been chasing spaces that don't actually serve me?

_____

_____

What does *alignment* look and feel like for me?

_____

_____

What would it look like to stop proving myself and start positioning myself?

_____

_____

What kind of rooms do I want to start building for others?

_____

_____

Don't just aim for visibility.
Aim for values.
Aim for truth.
Aim for rooms that see you, hear you, and support the version of you that doesn't shrink.

You deserve the *right* room.
And when it doesn't exist?
You create it.

For When I Need a Reminder

Use this space to write down the truths, wins, or

lessons you need to come back to when life gets loud.

_____

_____

_____

_____

_____

_____

_____

_____

_____

_____

_____

_____

_____

_____

_____

_____

Notes to Future Me

Write to the version of you that's still becoming. What do they need to hear from you today?

_____

_____

_____

_____

_____

_____

_____

_____

_____

_____

_____

_____

_____

_____

_____

_____

_____

When I Forget Who I Am

We all have those days. Use this page to remind yourself of what's real when your confidence wavers.

s

_____

_____

_____

_____

_____

_____

_____

_____

_____

_____

_____

_____

_____

_____

_____

_____

Things I'll Never Dim Again

Your light was never meant to be hidden. Make a list of what you're no longer apologizing for.

_____

_____

_____

_____

_____

_____

_____

_____

_____

_____

_____

_____

_____

_____

_____

_____

My Personal Check-In

How are you really doing? No filters. No fluff. Just honesty. This is your space to unpack, reflect, and breathe.

_____
_____
_____
_____
_____
_____
_____
_____
_____
_____
_____
_____
_____
_____
_____
_____

My Growth Looks Like This

Growth isn't always loud, sometimes it whispers. Jot down the small wins, mindset shifts, and brave moves you've made. **THEY MATTER!**

_____
_____
_____
_____
_____
_____
_____
_____
_____
_____
_____
_____
_____
_____
_____
_____

YOU DID THAT!!!!!!

Take a second and really let that sink in.
You just walked through a journey most people avoid facing yourself.
Telling the truth.
Letting go of what's been holding you back.
And giving yourself *permission* to grow into the version of you that's been waiting to break free.

That's not small. That's not surface-level. That's *real*.

And here's the thing this work doesn't end here.
This guide was never about a perfect finish. It was about a powerful start.
So keep going. Keep becoming.
Keep choosing you.

And if you ever feel stuck or need a reminder of what's inside you, come back to these pages.
Come back to your words.
Come back to your truth.

And if no one else tells you today

I'm proud of you. I see you. And I'm walking with you.

With love always,

Coach Dominique

Let's stay connected:

Instagram: @Coach_Dominique

Website: www.coachdominique.com

YouTube: The Coach Dominique Brand LLC

Bring Coach Dominique to Your School, University, or Event

The Personal Permission Slip™ Keynote Experience

Trusted by schools, colleges, and youth organizations, this high-impact keynote is more than just a speech, it's a wake-up call.

Coach Dominique delivers a dynamic, story-driven presentation that helps students:

- Take ownership of their voice and choices
- Build confidence rooted in identity, not popularity
- Break free from silence, self-doubt, and shame
- Leave feeling seen, heard, and supported

This message ignites the room and leaves a lasting mark on campus culture, student engagement, and school climate.

✉️ **To book Coach Dominique:**
Email: info@coachdominique.com

www.ingramcontent.com/pod-product-compliance
Lightning Source LLC
Chambersburg PA
CBHW071110090426
42737CB00013B/2563